I Am Woman
(Poems written by a woman)

by
Marianne Hulse

2014

Contents

Woman

I am so very nearly perfect,
Being with me can be hell,
And though I'm very rarely wrong,
When I am, I do it well.

Questions of Eternity

Woman, alive to every sense,
With spirits that have known no fence
Welcomes colour, sunshine and moonlight
Into her crystal orb of sight.

Rejoices in music and the song of birds,
Carols in season, poems bright with words.

And to her expansive sense of touch
Comes the world, babies, lovers, such
Is the strength of joy that she exudes
All are encompassed by her moods.

And from the warm ambrosial spice
Of the blossoms and fruits of Paradise
Are distilled and trailed with power
The gorgeous scents of field and flower.

This lovely Aphrodite does no toiling,
For how could man refrain from spoiling.
Untroubled in this state is she,
With questions of eternity.

Ironmongery

When I shop in B & Q
I always think of you.
As I wander through Homebase
I see the image of your face.
And when I go to Focus
I think of the time that broke us,
When I smell ironmongery
I feel alone, and hungry.

Scattered Thoughts

Broken shattered dreams
Lie in pockets of my mind,
In thought's meandering streams
Shards of them I find.

Sharp and piercing fragments
Snag and paralyse the scenes,
While I struggle for the balance
To sense what it all means.

Thrown Away

The socks you gave me,
With Right and Left on them,
Wore through at the heel,
And I threw them away,
But that doesn't mean,
I don't still miss them.

The gloves you gave me,
With snowmen appliqués,
Went into holes at the finger,
And I threw them away,
But that doesn't mean,
I don't still miss them.

The coat you gave me,
Was warm and comforting.
The sleeve was torn by wire,
I only use it in the garden,
But that doesn't mean,
I don't still miss it.

The life you gave me,
Where we shared so much,
Was worn, in holes, and torn,
And I threw it away.
But that doesn't mean,
I don't still miss you.

Over the coffee

Self subjugation, feminine game,
Women using sexual power,
Liberation lost its way,
Role models lack the shame.
Fight, my sisters, grow,
Work for status,
Show them how,
Rate us
Now.

Costing the dearth

The hurt is not borne without cost;
As you say: I am stronger than you.
You know not the days I have lost
When your words, to me, are not true.
I know how to deal with the loss,
And I drown the pain with red wine
And pretend I don't give a toss
When I know you are spinning a line.
On days when the skies weep for me
And I wait with my dearly bought hope;
I hide want, so you cannot see,
Nurse my ache – Oh, yes, I can cope.

Rising Bright

In the warm August night,
The harvest moon rising bright,
We'd swim naked in the sea,
Phosphorescence stirred would be,
On the beach the fire would burn,
To sandy towels we'd return,
Glow worms on the cliffs would shine,
In the days when you were mine.

Black potatoes set to bake,
From the ashes we would rake,
Singing softly, then more bold,
With abandon, the wine took hold,
As the dew fell on the sand,
Eyes would meet and flesh demand,
And lust then and love took course,
In the days when I was yours.

The Time

Not to be with friends
Not the company of strangers
Not to be alone
It's not that I want
I want
I want to spend the time with you.

Friends invite, but despite
Their kindness
It's not that politeness
That I want
I want
I want to spend the time with you.

To split a bottle
With your brown eyes
Open nuts and get merry
Is what I want
I want
I want to spend the time with you.

To watch the lights unfocus
Draw curtains on the night
Put logs on the fire
And share the want
I want
I want to spend the time with you.

How many beginnings

How many beginnings, how many starts
Are counted in the flowering of life?
Sperm enters the egg and fuses the parts
Which grow and expel amid strife.

How many starts, how many beginnings
Does a child make when rising to walk?
Crying and trying and tumblings,
Babbling and learning to talk.

How many beginnings, how many ends
For the infant starting at school?
Shoelaces tying and making new friends
Out and away, and playing it cool.

How many beginnings, how many starts
Do the young make before their first kiss?
The agony they suffer when giving their hearts,
The highs, and the lows, and the bliss.

How many starts, how many beginnings
Build maturity in making a home?
Nesting, and downswings, and blessings,
A place to be warm in the storm.

How many beginnings, how many ends,
Experienced, aging, afflicted?
There is no way of escaping the trends,
But finished is a word for perfected.

Shame

Bidden to write a poem about school
I felt a deep reluctance,
Recalling the rulers and the rule;
A miserable existence.
My Catholic junior school was cruel;
A culture of impatience.
Despite the diligence of our toil,
Punished for incompetence.
Labelled stupid, struck, and called a fool,
With sarcasm, torture and insistence.
Released to home, we never told the whole,
Ashamed was our acceptance.

Learning left from wrong?

Addressing letters, how to measure rain,
Right from left, tables, spelling
Inculculated with a cane,
Still my bitterness is welling.

I cannot tell left from right,
Cannot add or tell my tables now,
Lessons learned in times of fright,
Are not retained, but blocked somehow.

biological
The ⌃ imperative

You meet a man
And passion's hot
You want to go
To bed a lot.

And then you rage
With P.M.T.
I think I know
Why this should be.

Your body now
Attempts to say
You should be in
The family way.

Nature's message
Is to reject
This partner and
Again select.

Months of this
And you grow cold
Desire is lost
Which once was bold.

The imperative
Is a mate
Who with his seed
Can impregnate.

There is no proof

When people die where do they go?
I wish it were something we could know.
For if we knew without a doubt
What happens when the spark goes out,
Think what a comfort it would be
A finish to uncertainty.

The search of grief has no end,
We've truly lost and cannot send
A message through to those who've died.
Address unknown, though men have tried,
In myth, theology and invention
To explain a resurrection.
There is no proof that life remains,
However much the missing pains.

Bom

I still miss you very much
(Lying there in the road)
You know that it was such
(Blood trickling from your mouth)
A shock, you went so fast
(Ambulance came for you)
And all these years have passed
(We met at Casualty)
But it still wets the eyes
(David and James and I)
However hard one tries
(In the relatives room)
To hold on to the gladness
(They told us you were dead)
Your aging brought no sadness.

Sometimes

These are words that carry meaning,
'My husband' and 'my wife'
Of closeness and of partnering,
And companionship in life.

I like my girded isolation,
And not needing to account,
But when these words are spoken
I sometimes feel left out.

The Box

My aunt gave me a box,
Inside were curled locks
Of my mother's hair.
Shining, fine, and golden brown,
Sweetly coiled around,
Kept through the years with care.

She died nineteen years ago this May,
I remember her hair as grey
Unlike this young girls'.
I went to my sister's house and there,
Over the cups and the cafetiere,
Opened the box of curls.

It lay between us on the table,
I was relieved that she was able
To say we didn't have to keep it.
Cowardly, I left the box behind,
And hope she didn't mind
Acting as she thought fit.

I am full of cold

I am full of cold,
I wonder why we haven't found a cure,
I hear through stuffed up ears,
I see that no one gets too close,
I want a hot toddy,
I am full of cold.

I pretend it doesn't matter that much,
I feel bunged up,
I touch the roughened patches on my nose,
I worry that I will wet myself when I cough,
I cry, "I feel awful."
I am full of cold.

I understand the replication of viruses,
I say "Come on little lymphocytes, do your stuff."
I dream and remember them, because I keep waking up,
I try to reach the tissues before I sneeze,
I hope it won't last much longer,
I am full of cold.

Subtext

Tell me in a poem short
What would be your intention,
Should I entertain the thought,
And is it worth a mention?

Would you care to play with me?
Of the plot I am not sure,
I have a need to know, you see,
If your happiness is pure.

Surrender

Wetness with kisses start,
Feather breast, stirring inside,
Moving and laying apart,
Exposing, opening wide,
Want rises, mounts and quickens,
Touching down spine makes spasm,
Idly drawn through but thickens
Need to the edge of chasm,
Pushed, arching, rendered mute,
Only thought the urge to fill;
Power then is absolute,
Use it any way you will.

Unsure

You are so like him,
And I am so unsure
Of where he ends and you begin.
My hunger whets my need
And dulls my sense,
And instead of underground,
Where it still was wet,
I wanted wetness in
Your four-poster.

Lying Back

The little rape that many women
Know, and understand
When desire is lost and pinned beneath
The weight of the marriage band;
When forced by gilt, and duty bound,
Then love acts underhand.
Dissemble, rather than rest in peace;
Lest he should be unmanned.

The Catch

The boat lies beached on the gravel,
The couple on either side unravel
The heavy long net heaped inside,
Behind them, picked out and laid wide,
Folded clean over the clay blue beach
Netting. They stand and with both ands each
Adds to the weed that litters the shore,
With the increase of weed, more and more
Netting folds out on the blue clay.
The stink of the weed in the hot day,
Green and red, the weed tangles the net,
In the hot sun they pull out the wet
Weed, adding to that brought by the tide,
Red and green, lying on either side.
Working together, clearing weed caught,
Saying the catch amounted to naught.

Thorness Bay

Look out at the wide sweep of the bay,
The morning dark and the sea all grey.
As the day grows older sun breaks through
And turns the bay to a deep slate blue.
The trees and bushes of the hedgerow
Catch the sun and their autumn leaves glow.
The wet fields shine with spider trails,
The bay is patterned with white boat sails.
The day moves on and the sun sinks red,
Over the headland fire clouds are shed.
Evening darkens and makes the sea black,
The lights across the bay wink back.
Then silvered the bay by the moonlight,
Light up the stove and welcome the night.

"It's alright for you"

Who has a perfect life?
No worries, and a clear blue sky?
Show me a person with no strife,
I bet you can't - and that is why.

> Never say
> > "It's alright for you"
> Because, of course,
> > It isn't true.

Conviction

One man took lives,
Which were gladly given up
Because they were no longer wanted,
And he was called a criminal.

Many men took lives,
Wrecked and devastated homes
Because it was deemed necessary,
And they were called heroes.

Born upon the Road

Born upon the road, left bereft and helpless,
Parted from relations, mother lost to illness,
Dispossessed by war, injustice and unfairness.
      Does he have a birth right?

For men he has never met, and he has never harmed,
Forced his people from the land they had always farmed,
Fearful and bewildered, they had fled unarmed.
      Does he have a birth right?

Raised without state in the company of strangers,
A child on his own is prey to many dangers,
Each day he grows knowing how to nurse his angers.
      Does he have a birth right?

Careless men who oppressed with wealth and with
                         power,
Have nurtured well the hate, that then comes to flower,
And will they harvest dread, in his time, in his hour.
      Does he have a birth right?

      Does he have a birth right?

Who

When I pick up my sewing,
Who tugs the threads from my lap?
Who leaps onto my stomach,
When I settle for a nap?
Cat.

When I have finished cleaning,
Who sheds fur around the house?
Who leaves a present on the stairs,
So I tread upon a mouse?
Cat.

When I've just filled the larder,
Who disdains her favourite food?
Who, if I try to brush her,
Spits and stalks off in a mood?
Cat.

When I have just got settled,
Who scratches to go outside?
Who now wants to be back in,
And my patience, who, has tried?
Cat

When times are hard and lonely,
Who purrs and lies here curled?
Who listens to my troubles?
I'd not change her for the world.
Cat.

Lanyard Shipling

If you can keep the tune when all about you
Are losing it and singing out of key;
If you've a mind to sing and there's no doubt you
Know many, many songs about the sea;
If you can drink and not be tired by quaffing,
And still sing after supping all the night;
If you forget the words and come up laughing,
Or can remember half the verses right;

If you can sing and drink, and drink and sing,
And drink and sing, and drink, and sing and drink;
If you can do that John Kanaka thing,
Despite the fifteen pints you sink;
If you know your capstan from your captain,
And can sing at length about each one;
If you can sing the parts between refrain,
And if you know the place where Tom has gone;

If you can sustain a pumping rhythm,
And know the words to Albertina too;
If you knew Johnny Collins, and could sing with him,
Or form part of a landlocked crew;
If you can shorthaul past your forebit,
And down Sea Fever bitter by the tun –
Yours is the Minerva, and all that's in it
And – which is more – you'll be a shanty man, my son.

Post Festival Blues

I woke up this morning
And packed my tent away,
Said goodbye to Warwick
In the middle of the day.
But now I've got
The post festival blues.

It's not a healthy lifestyle;
Singing late at night,
But if I won the lottery
Then I know I might
Not have to get
Those post festival blues.

I'd become an old age traveler
And buy a camping van,
Spend the summer on the road,
Not in thrall to any man.
Now I've just got
The post festival blues.

The beer in my tankard
Doesn't taste the same at home;
I want to be an aged hippie
And the music sites to roam.
And now I've got
These post festival blues.

With Tom Lewis and Johnny Collins,
Dave and Anni too
We shared the rousing chorus
Until the day was new.
But now I've got
Deep post festival blues.

I know that there'll be other times
As glorious as this,
Beer, lazy sunshine, and the song
And getting fairly pissed.
I just can't shake
These post festival blues.

Some Sing

Some sing to feed their ego,
And some to entertain,
Some singers make your spirits grow,
But others should refrain.

You know how it is, when you've been on the piss,
And all you want is a bloody good sing,
With a group that's carousing, with choruses rousing,
And making the rafters to ring.

It's all going well, and the feeling is swell,
Then someone presents a miserable ballad,
And curses, oh, curses, it's got twenty three verses
And a tune that's unutterably sad.

A chance to recover, but no, here comes another,
A dreary thirteen verse spouting.
In their place they are good, but really they should
Not be given a festival outing.

It only needs the wild rover, and the whole thing is over,
The best singers have drifted away.
The damage is done, the ambience gone,
And I guess one only can say

Some sing to feed their ego,
And some to entertain,
Some singers make your spirits grow,
But others should refrain.

With affection

Our Jim's a jewel of a man,
He makes music whenever he can;
When he belts out a song
The words may be wrong
But then, some of my poems don't scan.

Occasionally words he may alter,
But he does it with barely a falter,
He hums I have heard
When he loses a word,
I'm sure that you'll note it hereafter.

You'd find many things that he's anti,
His regard for nature is scanty,
He's pro a fixed link,
And fond of a drink,
But he is your man for a shanty.

Coat

My brother had an afghan,
No, not the sort that's hound,
And it hummed so fiercely,
It should have made a sound.

He'd sprayed it with patchouli,
A scent I can't abide,
And it smelled so strongly,
My mother made it live outside.

You could smell him from a distance,
Of half a mile or so,
And anywhere my brother went,
The afghan was sure to go.

His hair was long and curly,
And the coat was muddy brown,
It went with him to festivals,
It should have been put down.

But, those were days of freedom,
For my brother, and for me,
And when I smell patchouli
I think of him you see.

So, when I saw this coat,
Hanging there for sale,
Those days came back to meet me,
I took it off the rail.

I tried on the past,
And asked what she would take.
I parted with the money –
An afghan for old times sake.

Depression

So many empty spaces,
So many voids to fill.
One step forward, and back two paces
And the hurt inside me still.
Crawling deep in the abyss,
Dim and dour the light.
Contact, converse with others miss
Alone inside my night.
Speaking out to a stranger,
And at a loss for words
To explain the sense of danger
The world for me begirds.
Seeking for an ending,
Longing that it might be passed.
Taking life is where it's tending;
Over then at last.

Disturbance

Take a calm pool
Ruffled at times
By passing events
At equilibrium.
Throw in a boulder
And watch the turbulence
Mud stirred into water
The disturbance
And wreckage
Of the surface
And the banks
And the depths
So it is with me.

Ducks

The enthusiasm of ducks
Is a cause for wonder.
There is nothing half hearted
About a duck.

Clear clean water
Savoured in the beak.
Plunge in and dabble,
Duck and dive.

Water off a ducks back,
Feathers oiled and ordered,
Shivered into place
In barbed patterns.

Fervour in the hunt
Through grass and shrubs;
Digging muddy holes,
Eager for new turned earth.

Good weather for ducks;
Soft, moist, worm laden.
Slugs and snails digested
Into eggs.

Mucky ducks.

Hairdressing

I deemed it wise, with hair at my eyes,
To call in and get a trim.
The stylist looked at what else was booked,
And said she could fit me in.

I expect hairdressing is tough,
With standing about all the day,
The skin on your hands must get rough
With the use of shampoos and spray.

I sat in the chair while she looked at my hair,
And she said with faintest reproof,
"It's got very long. Perhaps I am wrong,
But have you cut it yourself?"

I expect hairdressing is tough,
With standing about all the day,
And as if that wasn't enough –
There's thinking of something to say.

My hair wet and flat, she started to chat,
"Have you been abroad yet this year?"
She snipped away, and talked holiday,
While water itched in my ear.

I expect hairdressing is tough,
With standing about all the day,
And using the dryer to puff
Shape into hairs gone astray.

Each time I am sure, if I only knew more,
I could ask for a stunning style.
The usual cut is adequate but
I'd like to look great for a while.

I expect hairdressing is tough,
With standing about all the day,
Do you think she knows I will bluff
When she asks me, "Is it okay?"

Downbeat

-Just say no.
 -Don't go with the flow.
 - And give no indication
 - Of the depth of your disinclination.
 - - Until at the point of no return,
 - - - You make savage complaint.
 - - - And spoil
 - - - - For all.
 - - - - - With the desperation
 - - - - - Caused by realisation
 - - - - - - That we got it
 - - - - - - - So wrong.

Hello Grief

Hello Grief, my old friend,
How well I do remember you,
Mine the beginnings, yours the end,
I plant the shoots, you tend the rue.

In my heart

Because grieving is so grim
I long for levity;
So the words that make you grin
Blanket my gravity.

Shifting Sand

Untruths muddy the waters,
Create guilt within your soul,
Your feeling toward me falters,
Confession might make you whole.

I sense the murky confusion,
Uncertain of where I stand,
Knowing that there's a deception,
Feet planted in shifting sand.

Settle the swirls in our mind,
By saying outright what is true,
Honesty would be more kind,
Hide not, you know I love you.

Security

The assurances you want from me
Cannot be forthcoming;
You want security, you see
And I have no way of knowing
What the future holds.
I simply live from day to day,
I can't keep you from the colds
Of the winds of change
Whatever I may say.

All at Sea

I wish that you would talk to me,
I have wrecked myself on your rocks.
The beacon shone out plain to see.
There's no kind harbour, no safe docks.

I, drawn like a moth to the light,
Not believing in the breakers,
Now I'm drowning in the night.
Of our fates, are we the makers?

My life has been forever marked.
I heeded not the warning bell.
The fire you kindled only sparked,
And inflamed my empty shell.

2000

I thought it didn't matter,
That it was just a date,
I would spend it quietly,
And not arrange to celebrate.

But as the time approached,
I found that I was wrong
And wanted then with all my heart
To be in a party throng.

I had a glass of wine to see
New Zealand's new year in,
Another one with Sydney,
And watched their display begin.

Through the day I drank with all
The countries of the world,
As each one changed their digits,
And the century unfurled.

So I joined the global party,
And when the clock rolled over
I felt OK, but must admit,
I was not entirely sober.

New Year's Ceilidh

In the dance I saw the look
Of understanding, as you took
The steps around and well I knew
What passes here 'twixt me and you;
The glance that says I know you well,
Our mutual pride your eyes will tell,
The confidence that we exchange,
And reassurance, nothing strange.
The smiles that pass between us here
Say we have shared another year;
The spark of love between us such,
The joy of dancing moves me much.

New Year's Eve

You ask me for a poem, but
I tell you there's no chance.
I do not choose to speak tonight,
Tonight I want to dance!

Soul Mates

Meeting of another with an interest in common,
Meeting and talking and going out together,
Talking of places, books and the way that life has gone,
Exploring life's events, matching them with humour,
Laughter and moving slowly closer, touching on desire,
Desiring and closing the gap that lies between,
Friendship and intimacy, where passion lights a fire,
Coming then the evening that can only mean
Meeting moves to mating and is joyous in success,
Building understanding, a feeling that the fates
Having decreed, this is a union they will bless,
Smiling, for they recognize that these are soul mates.

For Ed

All the occasions of our meeting
Are set, jeweled and sparkling,
In my consciousness.
The words that we have exchanged,
The jokes and shared gifts
Are precious gems.
I will pour amber over each memory
So that whatever comes
The recollections are retained.
Sometimes
I will polish them.

Notes

Woman
This is, of course, a universal truth, and I'm not sure how many years it is since I wrote this one.

Questions of Eternity
Written in January 2003 after reading 'The Cage' by Martin Amstrong. His poem was written in 1925, and from the comparison I'd rather be the woman.

Ironmongery
Written in July 1999, other Hardware shops are available.

Scattered Thoughts
Written around 1995/6, I think, following a time when a long term relationship ended, I was therefore homeless and then redundancy meant that I lost my job. Oh, and someone stole my bicycle.

Thrown Away
Written around 1999. The coat has also been thrown away now, and I am over missing him.

Over the coffee
This is a nonet. It is a poem with nine lines and the first line has nine syllables. The second line has eight syllables, the third line has seven syllables. I'm sure you can work out the rest of the pattern.

This one was written in July 2012, over the coffee during a family dinner table discussion. These can get quite lively between the driver and my two step daughters.

(The driver – this is a reference to my book 'Travels on the A38' where the husband becomes the driver.)

Costing the dearth
In 1995/1996 I spent some time with a man who lied to me. I was astonished by the depth and complexity of the

lies as they were uncovered. I was still able to make puns though.

Rising Bright
Another pun? This one is a nostalgic look back to the evenings spent at Thorness Bay on the Isle of Wight, before everything fell apart on me (I have put it back together now).

The Time
Christmas Day alone, it isn't easy, but sometimes it is better than being with other people. Written in December 2001.

How many beginnings
December 2011. Why is it that as soon as you get the hang of life, parts of you stop working correctly? Despite that I am now perfected.

Shame
School, it wasn't a happy time. There was a great deal of cruelty in our classrooms, and I was eleven before it was realised how short sighted I was. I expect that I hadn't been able to see the board, or the teacher's face for some time.

I think that when I was very little I did try to tell my parents that it was a bad place. They had difficulties with me at the classroom door. But they didn't listen then, or so it seemed. We (me and my brothers and sisters) stopped telling them how dreadful it was, felt ashamed and just coped.

This poem and the one below were written in May 2012. I left school in the early 1970s.

Learning left from wrong
See above. Mental arithmetic and tables, these were almost as dangerous as spelling tests. I find working with numbers very difficult, and have to work everything out

from base. I just don't remember the answer to questions like what is 7 plus 5. But at college I did a maths module, and was extremely chuffed by the description that 'I was a fine mathematician in my own right'. I'm not entirely sure what that meant, but I love patterns and working with algebra and number sequences. I just can't add up, or tell left from right.

The *biological* imperative
Pre-menstrual tension. Does it exist? Or does everyone in the world (especially the men in your life) become exceptionally irritating in the week before you have your monthlies? Perhaps it has a purpose.

I'm not sure when I wrote this one, probably before 1994.

There is no proof
Death. Some people reading this poem have tried to tell me that there is a proof, that they have belief in heaven.

I wrote this poem after the death of Beth Fender, in November 2002. Beth was an inspiration and a friend and her memory lives on in **Beth's Poetry Trail** in Belper, Derbyshire. You can find out more about Beth and the Poetry Trail at http://www.bethspoetrytrail.co.uk/trail.html

I feel that I have lost people, I don't know where they are. I'll wait, one day I may know the answer...

Bom
When we had children, our mother became known as Bom, which was a contraction of the Dutch/Flemish word Bonmama (grandma).

She died suddenly, with a brain hæmorrhage while she was cycling home from church. She wasn't far from home, and I went to the roadside before the ambulance came.

Sometimes
November 2001 – I was living alone, and this sums up just exactly how I felt at the time.

The Box
If you have a box full of your sister's teenage hair, give it back to her. Don't keep it to burden her children with in the future.

The poem was written in April 2003.

I am full of cold
'I am' poems are a strange phenomena. They are written to a template, with a prompt at the start of each line. Every time I have written one of these they emerge quite different in the language, tone and sentiments expressed.

Are they really poems?

The 'I am poem' follows this template...

I am (two special characteristics)
I wonder (something you are actually curious about)
I hear (an imaginary sound)
I see (an imaginary sight)
I want (an actual desire)
I am (the first line of the poem restated)

I pretend (something you actually pretend to do)
I feel (a feeling about something imaginary)
I touch (an imaginary touch)
I worry (something that really bothers you)
I cry (something that makes you very sad)
I am (the first line of the poem repeated)

I understand (something you know is true)
I say (something you believe in)
I dream (something you actually dream about)
I try (something you really make an effort about)
I hope (something you actually hope for)

I am (the first line of the poem repeated)

...but I don't always strictly follow the instructions.

This is a cold that I was infected with in January 2014.

Subtext
You know how it is when you first meet someone, and you are both interested and it is a very flirty time...

Surrender
... and then you move on to a more physical phase.

Unsure
Probably too much information already.

Lying Back
Sometimes you might not want to make love, but the other person does. Sometimes you acquiesce and it all turns out well.

In no way should this poem be taken to condone rape in any circumstances. I'm talking about consent freely given here.

The Catch
When we were children on the Isle of Wight we regularly watched a couple cleaning the nets on the beach after a fishing trip. We had great affection for these people, who always had a kind word for us.

Thorness Bay
This is the most beautiful place in the world. Well there may be others, but for me it is heart-achingly lovely.

"It's alright for you"
This is a very annoying phrase. I wrote this little sermon in March 2001.

Conviction
I wrote this around the time of the 2003 invasion of Iraq, after reading about people who were criminalised for assisting someone with a terminal illness to take their own lives.

Born upon the Road
This poem came from thinking about why people do terrible things, and why there is such hatred. It was originally written as a lyric.

Who
Cats!

Lanyard Shipling
This parody was written for the Hull Sea Fever Festival, which used to be a glorious free festival at the side of the River Humber.

There are a number of references to the words of Sea Shanties in the poem, 'The Albertina' is a pumping shanty and 'Tom's gone to Hilo'.

Johnny Collins died in 2009, he was a unique and wonderful singer.

The Minerva is a pub on the pier head in Hull. They used to sell 'Sea Fever' bitter during the festival, and when the shanty crews and singers were packed into the front room and singing, there was no better place to be.

Post Festival Blues
The Warwick Folk Festival. Some great singing, well into the night.

Tom Lewis is a fine singer songwriter. Dave Webber and Anni Fentiman sing together, Dave writes lovely songs, and they are also favourites of mine.

Some Sing
It doesn't always go well when you try to organise a singing session at a festival.

With Affection
This was written with affection about Jim Jewel who ran the Isle of Wight folk club (and also the Starboard Watch shanty crew).

'a fixed link' – the debate about whether there should be a bridge or tunnel from the mainland to the Island.

Coat
A simple poem written for my brother (and the coat) written in August 2000.

Depression
I have had a few bouts of depression in my life, the earliest I remember was when I was seventeen. It is like a heavy blanket falling in my mind, and I have tried to describe some of my feelings in this poem. It was written in 1995.

Disturbance
You just get everything on an even keel, and then something changes...

Ducks
I love my ducks. We have two Indian Runner ducks who help to keep the garden in order. I tried to use clichés about ducks in this poem, as they are all true.

Hairdressing
Do you bluff too?

Downbeat
This one is written about our father. He was a difficult man for us to know. He was quite distant, and then suddenly he would shout at us. I was anxious around him.

Written December 2012, thirty two years after his death.

Hello Grief
For about five years after our mother died I was devastated with grief. I recovered, but small losses (the death of a duck) bring back these feelings.

In my heart
Just don't assume that because you smile at my words that I find things funny.

Shifting Sand
See the notes made for 'Costing the dearth'. I should have walked away.

Security
As above. But you never know what the next day holds.

All at Sea
At last, I begin to see sense.

2000
The turn of the century, I was on my own.

New Year's Ceilidh
Written around 1997, this describes happier times before 1994.

New Year's Eve
Sometimes during the Ceilidh we used to have floor spots where someone would sing or recite. This was one of my contributions.

Soul Mates

Written in September 2002. Eventually it all comes right and you meet someone with whom you would like to spend the rest of your life.

For Ed

I have put my dedication at the end of the book. This is for my husband, who is a patient man (most of the time) and also is the driver and helmsman in our adventures.

I AM WOMAN

8019099R00028

Printed in Great Britain
by Amazon.co.uk, Ltd.,
Marston Gate.